P9-DUS-525

Teaching Children
Compassionately

How Students and Teachers Can
Succeed with Mutual Understanding

*A Nonviolent Communication™
presentation and workshop transcription by*
Marshall B. Rosenberg, Ph.D.

PuddleDancer
P R E S S

P.O. Box 231129, Encinitas, CA 92023-1129
email@PuddleDancer.com • www.PuddleDancer.com

For additional information:
Center for Nonviolent Communication, 2428 Foothill Blvd., Suite E, La Crescenta, CA 91214
Tel: 818-957-9393 • Fax: 818-957-1424 • E-mail: cnvc@CNVC.org • Website: www.CNVC.org

ISBN: 1-892005-11-5

© Copyright 2005 PuddleDancer Press
Published by arrangement with the Center for Nonviolent Communication. All rights reserved.
No part of this booklet may be reproduced by any means, nor may it be stored,
transmitted or otherwise copied without permission of the publisher.

Language of the Heart

A Heart to Heart Talk

Language of the Heart

Introduction

The following is excerpted from a 1999 Keynote Address to the National Conference of Montessori Educators, given by Marshall Rosenberg in San Diego, California. In it he describes the basic features of Nonviolent Communication (NVC), and offers illustrations of how they might be used in school, at work, and in everyday life. In particular, Marshall describes the language of giraffes and jackals, the vocabulary of feelings and needs, the difference between observation and evaluation and between requests and demands, the role of power, punishment, and the vital skill of empathic connection.

In many countries Nonviolent Communication is popularly known as "Giraffe Language." Marshall picked the Giraffe, the land animal with the largest heart, as a symbol for NVC, a language that inspires compassion and joyful relationships in all areas of life. As a language that stresses the expression of feelings and needs, NVC invites vulnerability and transforms it into strength.

Marshall often uses a Jackal puppet to represent that part of ourselves that thinks, speaks, or acts in ways that disconnect us from our awareness of our feelings and needs, as well as the feelings and needs of others. "Jackal" language makes it very hard for a person who uses it to get the connection they want with others, making life much less wonderful than it otherwise could be. The NVC practice is to recognize and befriend "Jackals" by receiving those less-than-life-enriching thoughts and habits compassionately—and free from moral judgment—while we retrain ourselves to experience life in increasingly more wonderful ways. In this booklet the word "Giraffe" is used interchangeably with NVC—and may also refer to a practitioner of NVC—while "Jackal" refers to thinking and speaking in ways that do not reflect the practices of NVC.

●   ●   ●

On Jackals and Giraffes

This is a great thrill for me to be here today and share some ideas with you. I'm glad to do it to give something back, because I'm very grateful for what my children received from Montessori education. They received many gifts. One of the gifts they received was to be exposed at a very young age to other languages. And I don't think it's accidental that as a result of that my oldest son is now head of a language program teaching English as a Second Language in Sao Paulo, Brazil, and my youngest son is now about to get his doctorate in Spanish, and will accompany me next month when we begin a new project in Colombia, as my translator. So it's a great joy for me to share with you some things that I hope will contribute to your teaching and your personal lives as well.

I'm interested in learning that's motivated by reverence for life, that's motivated by a desire to learn skills, to learn new things that help us to better contribute to our own well-being and the well-being of others.

And what fills me with great sadness is any learning that I see motivated by coercion. By coercion I mean the following: Any student that's learning anything out of a fear of punishment, out of a desire for rewards in the form of grades, to escape guilt or shame, or out of some vague sense of "ought" or "must" or "should." Learning is too precious, I believe, to be motivated by any of these coercive tactics.

So I have been interested in studying those people that have the ability to influence people to learn, but learning again that is motivated by this reverence for life, and not out of some coercive tactics.

And one of the things that I've found by studying such people is that they spoke a language that helps people to learn motivated by reverence for life. As I've studied people who have this ability, I've noticed that they spoke a different language than the language that I was educated to speak. And this language that contributes to helping people learn by reverence for life I call, officially, Nonviolent Communication. But for fun and teaching purposes I like calling it "Giraffe Language."

Unfortunately, giraffe language is not the language that I was educated to speak. I did not go to Montessori schools. I went to "jackal" schools. And in jackal schools, as you might guess, the teachers spoke the language of jackal, not the language of giraffe. I hope none of you have ever heard the language of jackal. I wish it were outlawed in all schools throughout the world, but the teachers at the schools I went to spoke jackal.

So let me give you an idea of what a jackal-speaking teacher sounds like. Let's imagine that you are my students and I'm the teacher, and I happen to observe one of you doing something that's not in harmony with my values. I see you sitting at your seat, and instead of doing what I'm asking the class to do, you're drawing a picture of me with a knife in my back and blood spurting out.

Now, how do I evaluate you if I am a jackal-speaking teacher? It's obvious: You're emotionally disturbed. This is how jackal-speaking people have been trained to think. When there is a conflict, they think in terms of what is wrong with the person who's behaving in a way that is in conflict with their values.

Or let's say that you don't understand something I've said. "You're a slow learner." But what if you say some things that I don't understand? "You're rude and socially inappropriate."

What if I speak so rapidly you can't follow me? "You have an auditory problem." What if you speak so rapidly I can't follow you? "You have an articulation problem."

So you see, jackal education is a very strange experience. Let me give you an example of what happens in jackal schools. Imagine that you are a car salesman. And you're not selling any cars. Well, you fire the customers. That might seem like a strange experience, but in the jackal schools that I went to, that's what happened. This language of jackal was the primary language used. And if you didn't measure up, you were not promoted, not rewarded, and so forth.

So I saw that the language that really helped people to teach in a way that I valued was a very different language from the language that I was educated to speak. And why did I call it giraffe language? Well, giraffes have the largest heart of any land animal. And, as I'll try to show you in our time together this morning, the language of Nonviolent Communication is a language of the heart. It requires knowing how to speak always from your heart, and since giraffes have the largest heart of any land animal, what better name for a language of the heart than "giraffe?"

Now, let me share with you this language of giraffe, or Nonviolent Communication, and I'll try to show you how it might apply in conflict resolution with students, or with other teachers or parents.

NVC requires us to be continually conscious of the beauty within ourselves and other people. There's a song I'd like to sing for you to help get us in the mood for understanding the mechanics of Nonviolent Communication. I would guess that many of you might already be familiar with this song. It was written by a couple named Red and Kathy Grammer, and some of the Montessori schools I've been working with lately have been using their music for teaching purposes. But I find that people I work with all over the world like this song. It's a song called, "See Me Beautiful."

"See Me Beautiful"
Look for the best in me
That's what I really am
And all I want to be
It may take some time
It may be hard to find
But see me beautiful

See me beautiful
Each and every day
Could you take a chance

Could you find the way
To see me shining through
In everything I do
And see me beautiful [1]

So Nonviolent Communication is a way of keeping our consciousness tuned in moment by moment to that beauty within ourselves and others, and not saying anything that we think might in any way tarnish people's consciousness of their own beauty. Nonviolent Communication shows us a way of being very honest, but without any criticism, without any insults, without any putdowns, without any intellectual diagnosis implying wrongness. Because the more we use words that in any way imply criticism, the more difficult it is for people to stay connected to the beauty within themselves.

And Nonviolent Communication shows us a way of staying with that beauty in ourselves and with other people, even when *they* are not using Nonviolent Communication.

One of my happiest days as a parent was when the first of my children went to a non-Montessori school. My oldest son, Rick, when he was 12, had graduated from the Montessori school, and now he was going for the first day to a school in our neighborhood. And I was wondering what it was going to be like for him, after spending his first six years in quite a different school.

So when he came home the first day I said, "Hey, Rick, how was the new school?" He was "underwhelmed." He said, "It's okay, Dad, but boy, some of those teachers." I said, "What happened?"

He said, "Dad, I wasn't even in the front door of the school, really, I was like halfway through the front door, and some man teacher comes running over to me and says, 'My, my, look at the little girl.'" You can probably guess what the teacher was reacting to. My son had hair down to his shoulders. Now, in a jackal school the teachers think that authority knows what's right. Isn't that a primitive idea? And they think the way to motivate people is through insults and criticism, to motivate by guilt and shame. So this was my son's introduction to the other world. So I said, "How did you handle it?"

He said, "I remembered what you said, Dad, that when you're in that kind of institution, never give them the power to make you submit or rebel." And I couldn't have been more thrilled as a parent than that he had remembered that abstract but important message under those conditions. Never give people, or the institutions within which we live, the power to make you submit or rebel. So I said, "Well, gosh, I'm pleased that you remembered that. And how did you react to his statement?"

"Well," he said, "Dad, I again did what you suggested that we do. I put on my giraffe ears." Now this technology is superb, because it helps us to see the beauty in other people, regardless of their language. We don't allow their words, or how they are communicating, to take us into a world that we don't want to be in.

So as soon as we turn these ears on, that's all we can hear. We don't hear what's coming out of a person's mouth or their head. We see what's in their heart.

So I said to him, "Well, gosh, again it makes me very pleased, Rick, that you remembered to try to hear the teacher in a human way when he was speaking that way." Now, with these ears, all we can hear are feelings and needs, you see. That's what's in there, always, behind every message. That's the basic vocabulary, the basic literacy of Nonviolent Communication: feelings and needs.

And you learn to hear the feelings and needs behind any message. So I said, "What did you hear when you put on your ears and you tried to hear his feelings and needs?" He said, "It was pretty obvious, Dad. I heard that he was feeling irritated, and probably wanted me to get my hair cut."

I said, "How did it leave you feeling?" He said, "Dad, I felt sad for the man. He was bald and seemed to have a problem about hair."

I was working with some eighth graders not long ago in the state of Washington, and I was showing them the trick that my son was demonstrating there. We were practicing to put these ears on. And they were telling me several things that their parents and teachers were saying that were hard to hear with these ears. And I was showing them how to connect with the beauty, to see the beauty in them.

And I said, "Now as soon as you put these ears on, you will

always hear the jackal singing the same song, 'See Me Beautiful.'"
I've gotten some feedback. I've created monsters in that school.
Now the teachers tell me, whenever they scream at the children,
they put their arms around each other and sing, "See Me Beautiful."

Again, that's the basic vocabulary of Nonviolent
Communication: feelings and needs. There are a couple of other
ingredients, too, but if you can learn to speak to feelings and
needs, then it's easier for other people to see our humanness. It's
easier for them to see the beauty in us. And when we are living
Nonviolent Communication, all we can see is the feelings and
needs of the other person.

Observation vs. Evaluation

I'm suggesting today that we never evaluate a student's
performance by any jackal language. Let's get the following words
out of our consciousness as teachers: right, wrong, good, bad,
correct, incorrect, slow learner, fast learner. This is dangerous
language.

Some teachers in one school system I was working with in the
United States couldn't imagine going through one day without
using words that classify—right, wrong, good, bad, correct,
incorrect. And they said, "How are we to evaluate performance?"
They wanted me to show them how to do this using Nonviolent
Communication. So I took over several classes for the day
ranging from math classes to English to art classes, and they
followed me around with a video camera so that this could be
used to show the teachers how to evaluate performance in giraffe
language rather than in jackal language. They had about four
hours of videotape that we made. But this school system told me
that they'd only used the first ten minutes for teachers training.
They said, "That's all we need, Marshall, to make the point. What
happened in that first ten minutes was more than enough to
convince our teachers to learn giraffe language and not to go into
the class with jackal language."

Now, what happened in that first ten minutes? I came across
a young boy about age nine, and he had just finished adding up
a page of arithmetic problems, and I saw one of his answers was
nine plus eight equals fourteen. We all know it's seventeen.

And I said to him, "Hey, buddy, I'm confused about how you got that answer. I get a different one. Could you show me how you got that?" That's how to evaluate something like that in giraffe language.

Here's what happened. He looks down at the floor, and tears come to his eyes. And I said, "Hey, buddy, what's going on?" He said, "I got it wrong." See, already by the third grade he had learned to wear jackal ears, so that even if somebody else is speaking from the heart, he hears that he did something wrong. And it was quite clear that he not only had this word "wrong" in his consciousness, but you could see the shame he felt that to be wrong meant that "I must be stupid." That's another jackal concept: that there's such a thing as smart people and stupid people. Good questions and dumb questions.

So when we train people to hear criticism and negative judgment, any kind of learning is about as much fun as a prolonged dental appointment. Hearing criticism in what people say, or worrying about what people think of you—whether you are smart or dumb, right or wrong—has terrible effects on how we see ourselves. We don't see ourselves as beautiful. We can't.

Schooling teaches us—and taught me—to dehumanize human beings by thinking of *what* they are. And so I've been working very hard to develop this other language that helps me to stay connected to the beauty in people.

Now, let me show you what that language looks like. I'm going to ask you to think of somebody at the moment who is behaving in a way that is not making life particularly beautiful for you. This could be somebody at school. It could be somebody at home. It could be a child, a student, it could be one of your own children, or a parent, or another teacher. Or maybe you live at home with a jackal-speaking child who says horrible jackal things such as, "No!" Or maybe you from time to time are talked to by a parent or another teacher that says, "The problem with you is that you are too (fill in the blank)."

Okay, so think of a real situation, and then I'd like you to write down the answer to this question: *What is one specific action that this person takes that makes life less than wonderful for you?*

Now, I asked that question to the staff of a school in San

Francisco. The superintendent of the schools asked me to work with the staff because there was a lot of conflict between the staff and the principal of the school. I was going to meet first with the teachers and see if I could find out what was going on, and then get the teachers and administrator together to see if we couldn't make life more enjoyable for everyone.

So I asked the teachers that question I just asked you. Tell me one thing that the principal did that made it less than wonderful to work around him? And here's the first answer I got. One of the gentlemen said, "He has a big mouth."

You can see the difference between the question I asked and the answer I got. I asked for an observation, a specific behavior. I got back an evaluation. This is typical of jackal language. The people who speak this language have trouble separating observation and evaluation.

So I pointed out to this gentleman that what he answered was not the answer to my question. I was asking for an observation, and he was stuck. He couldn't think of how to say it without mixing in an evaluation. The woman next to him tried to help. She said, "Well, I know what he's talking about." "What is that?" I said. "The principal talks too much."

Now, the word "too" is a jackal favorite. This is how jackal people think, how their minds have been shaped to see the world. In their world there's a "just right," a "too much," and a "too little" for everything. And that's what makes them dangerous: They think they know what's right.

So I pointed out again that "too much" was an evaluation, and I was asking for an observation. Another teacher said, "He thinks only he has anything worth saying." "No," I said, "Telling me what you think he thinks is an evaluation. I'm asking for an observation."

Now this entire staff of highly educated people was silent. They couldn't answer the question. And then one woman said, "Boy, Marshall, that's hard to do." I said, "Yes, especially if you were taught to speak jackal like I was. It's very hard to separate observation and evaluation."

In fact, the Indian philosopher Krishnamurti says that the highest form of human intelligence is the ability to observe without evaluating. So with much help on my part, the staff was finally able to make a clear observation. Now, what was this? There were several of them, but the one that bothered them the most was this: During their weekly staff meetings, instead of staying with the agenda, this principal would tell war stories and childhood experiences, and as a result the average meeting lasted about 20 minutes longer than it was scheduled.

So I said to the staff, "Have any of you brought this to his attention?" And they said, "Well, we're afraid that if we try to talk to him about it, we'll mix in a lot of evaluations and he'll get defensive." So they thought it would be a good idea to talk to him about this, but they asked if I would be at the meeting just in case. And as it turned out, I'm glad I was at the meeting. Almost as soon as the staff meeting started, I saw exactly what they meant. Something would be raised, and the principal would say, "That reminds me of a time . . ." and I was waiting for somebody to tell him about that behavior and how it was not to their liking. But instead of speaking giraffe, I saw a lot of nonverbal jackal being spoken. For example, they were rolling their eyes, poking the person next to them, yawning, looking at their watches, holding their watches up to their ears. And they were electronic watches, so I don't know!

Finally I said, "Isn't somebody going to say something?" And then the man who spoke up in our first meeting began to get red in the face, getting his courage up. Then he looks at the principal and says, "Ed, you have a big mouth." So much for my teaching ability!

So take a look at what you wrote down. Is it a clear observation, or did you mix in some evaluation? And I'd like to hear several of you read them out loud, so that we can learn from it.

(Picking someone from the audience) Yes, what did you write down?

"He yells."

Maybe this story will help you understand why I wouldn't call "He yells" an observation. In a school in San Francisco I was asked by the superintendent to work with the faculty because there had been a lot of racial tension amongst the different cultural groups. I asked the faculty to tell me one thing that another faculty member does that they didn't like. A gentleman immediately looked at the woman next to him and said, "I don't like it when you yell in faculty meetings." And she said, "Who yells?" Now they were from two different cultures. And she didn't consider that yelling. And about ten minutes later when she started to yell at him by her own definition, I clearly saw a difference. "Yells" depends on how you hear it, so we would need to say something like "raises voice above the others." That would be an observation.

(Picking someone from the audience) Yes. (Question from audience) "So when he doesn't get what he wants, he screams and cries." Very observable. I'm glad that we didn't mix in dangerous language like "handles aggression in an immature way." We don't want to have in our head that there is such a thing as an immature child.

(Picking someone from the audience) Yes. I'm glad you caught that—"refuses to cooperate"—because I would have had to object twice there, first for the "refuses" and second for the word "cooperate." I would agree with "Does not do what I want." Notice how this requires us to be much more honest about what's going on?

Any others? (Picking someone from the audience) Yes. "Interrupts the group" is what she said. Now that's an embarrassing one for me. Let me show you why. Once I was trying to demonstrate how to do this process in front of a very large group of teachers, and they had some students on the stage for me to work with. Now, here was the observable behavior. There were three successive times where I was talking when one of the students started to talk before I finished. So that was the observation. He started to talk before I finished. And I said, "You know I get frustrated when you interrupt me." And another student said, "He's not interrupting, he's helping." This is a true story. I was very embarrassed. This young child caught me confusing observation and evaluation.

On "*Power*-With"

Now, I'm not suggesting by this that Nonviolent Communication requires us to be totally objective and to avoid any evaluation. Not at all, because the next steps involve evaluation. We're going to evaluate this behavior. But we're going to evaluate it in the way that has most power *with* people, not over them. You see,

Nonviolent Communication is based on a concept of power, power with people. We want people to do things because they see how it's going to enrich life. That's power-*with*–when we have the ability to motivate people from within. In contrast, power-*over* gets people to do things because of their fear of what we're going to do to them if they don't meet our demands, or how we will reward them if they do.

My own children have taught me very early in life the danger of power-*over* tactics. One of the first things they taught me is I couldn't make them do anything. I can't tell you what a helpful lesson that was. Somehow in my jackal background, I got it in mind that it was the job of a teacher or a parent to get people to do what's right. But here's this two year-old teaching me that no matter what I thought, I couldn't make them do anything. I couldn't even make them put the toy back in the toy box. "Please put the toy back in the toy box. We're going to go out now." "No." "Did you hear me?" "No." I couldn't make them do anything. All I could do is make them wish they had.

And then they taught me a second lesson about power. Any time I made them wish they had, they would make me wish I hadn't made them wish they had. Said more simply, violence begets violence. Any time I used violence to get my way, I would pay for it.

On Punishment and Violence

So let me suggest several kinds of violence that we want to avoid. First is the violence of any punishment. Let's strive for no punishment from this point on. Punishment is at the root of violence on our planet. There are ways of maintaining social rules and regulations that do not involve any kind of punishment. If we ask two questions of ourselves, we will see that punishment never works.

First question: What do we want the other person to do? Now, if we ask only that question, one can make an argument for punishment. You can probably think of times when you know that somebody was influenced to do something either by being punished for what they had done or out of a threat of punishment. However, when we add the second question, we see that punishment never works.

What is the second question? What do we want the other person's reasons to be for doing as we request?

Now for most people raised in our culture, they can't imagine what a world would look like without punishment. They have horrible images of anarchy, chaos, a world where nothing would ever get done. It's a hard concept to let go of until you really get clear about those two questions. If you don't get clear about those two questions, you can often end up thinking punishment works when it really doesn't.

For example, I was sitting in the office of a friend of mine, a principal of a school in San Francisco, where I was doing some work. He was looking out on the playground and he said, "Excuse me, Marshall." And he runs out and he grabs a big boy who was hitting a smaller boy, hit the bigger boy and said, "I'll teach you not to hit people who are smaller than you!" He's a good friend of mine, so I could tease him a bit, and when he returned to the office I said, "You know, I don't think you taught that student what you thought you were teaching him." He says, "What do you mean?" "You said you were going teach him not to hit smaller people, but you're bigger than he is, and you hit him. It looks to me like you were reinforcing the idea that it's okay to punish if you think you're right and you're big enough to punish." He said, "I never thought of that." I said, "But I do think you taught him something." "Yeah, what?" "I think you taught him not to hit smaller people while you were looking."

You see, if we're real clear about what punishment teaches, I'm confident we will never use punishment. We will use other forms of getting order in schools, and in society in general.

So punishment is one form of violence. A second form of violence is rewards. And if you have trouble digesting that, I suggest you read a book called, *Punished by Rewards* by Alfie Kohn, to see the violence of rewards.

Guilt is a form of violence as I define violence. We don't allow punishment by guilt in Nonviolent Communication schools we've created in different countries. These are disallowed tactics for resolving any differences. Punishment, reward, guilt. To play the guilt game you have to trick people into believing that they can create your feelings. So you have to learn how to play guilt games like this. "It really hurts me when you don't get your work done."

"You make me angry when you talk while I'm talking." The game of guilt is played when you try to convince people that they are the cause of your suffering. We'll show you other options to that game later on.

Another form of violence: any attempt to get people to do things out of shame. And we've already touched on that. It involves using labels so that if people don't do what you want, you put labels on them like "lazy," "inconsiderate," or "stupid." Any label that implies wrongness is a violent act. It's trying to get people to do things out of shame.

And perhaps the worst violence we can use in the role of an educator—according to my values—is the violence of "*Amtssprache*," which loosely translates into English as "office talk" or "bureaucratese." Why do I use that term? I borrow it from the Nazi war criminal Adolph Eichmann. At his trial for war crimes in Jerusalem, Eichmann was asked, "Was it hard for you to send tens of thousands of people to their deaths?" Eichmann said, "To tell you the truth, it was easy. Our language made it easy." That response shocked his interviewer, and his interviewer said, "What language?" Eichmann said, "My fellow Nazi officers and I had our own name of our language. We called it '*amptssprache*.' It's a language in which you deny responsibility for your actions. So if somebody asks you why you did what you did, you say "I had to." "Why did you have to?" "Superior's orders. Company policy. It's the law."

So here's classic *amptssprache,* the most dangerous words in the English language: have to, can't. And now here come some vulgar words. If you don't like vulgarity, close your ears: should, must, ought.

I said this once to a group of parents and teachers in St. Louis, Missouri, where I was working. One of the mothers got very upset at my suggesting that this was a violent language, this violence of *amptsprach*, a language that denies responsibility for choice. Here's what she said to me: "But there are some things that people have to do. It's our job as parents and teachers to teach our children what they have to do." She said, "There are things I have to do every day that I don't like to do, but I have to do them." I said, "Like what?" She said, "Well, for example, when I leave here tonight, I have to go home and cook. I hate to cook. I hate it with a passion. But I have done it every day for 20 years, even when I have been sick as a dog."

I told her I was very sad to hear that, because when we do any action through coercion, everybody pays for it. Now this woman was a very rapid learner. In fact, she went home that first night and announced to her family she no longer wanted to cook. And I got some feedback from her family.

The feedback came three weeks later when I was in the same community, and who shows up for an evening session that I was offering but her older two sons. They came up before the session and introduced themselves, and I said that I was glad to meet them, and I said, "You know, your mother has been calling me up it seems like every other day, telling me about these major changes she's been making in her life since she learned Nonviolent Communication, and I'm always wondering what that does to the rest of the family when one member comes home and starts speaking another language. What was it like that first night when she said she no longer wanted to cook?"

The oldest son, John, said to me, "Marshall, I just said to myself, 'Thank God!'" I said, "Help me understand why you say that." He said, "I said to myself, 'Now maybe she won't complain at every meal.'"

So you see, if we do anything motivated through coercion, everybody pays for it. Unless it's play, don't do it. And it will be play, even it means cleaning floors or toilets, if there are no coercive aspects and we see how it enriches life. But tell yourself "I should do it" and you won't. Or you'll hate doing it. Don't do anything you should, have to, must. Don't do it if it isn't play. And it'll be play if it serves life, and you see how it serves life. It'll be play even if it involves hard work.

So we want to evaluate in a way that allows people to learn without coercion. And to do that, Nonviolent Communication suggests that we evaluate people's behavior, not by any language that implies right and wrong, good and bad, not *amptssprache*, but a language of the heart, which I've already told you involves requiring us to be literate in expressing feelings and needs.

A Feeling Vocabulary

Let's look at feelings. I've asked you to identify a behavior that someone does that you don't like, that doesn't contribute to making life wonderful. Now I would like you to answer this question on a piece of paper. Write down how you feel when this behavior occurs. How do you feel when the person does this?

Let me hear a few of these. (Taking responses from the audience) Confused, yes. Uncomfortable, yes. Worried, yes. Lonely, angry, sad, yes. What was that? Inferior? Inferior is a self-judgment. It's what you think you are. It's more a mental concept of what you are. It doesn't really say how you feel. For example, I judge myself as inferior playing the guitar, but I enjoy playing it. So if I say I feel inferior playing the guitar, it doesn't tell you how I feel. I *feel* joy playing guitar. If you ask how I *judge* my ability, I would judge it as inferior.

Helpless, yes. Frustration, yes. Betrayed? No. Let me give you other, similar words so you can develop your ear and not confuse these words with feelings. The words I am about to say are not feelings, but are jackals in giraffe's clothing. Our language can enable us to pretend we're expressing feelings, but really what we're expressing is a judgment of the other person.

For example, "betrayed" doesn't say how you feel. It doesn't say whether you're hurt, sad, or angry. It says you have a mental image that this person is betraying you.

Here are some more words like that. I feel *misunderstood*. I feel *manipulated*. I feel *used*. I feel *criticized*. Again, I add, these are not feelings as I would define them. These are more mental images of what other people do, and more likely to cause problems than really to connect us at the heart level.

My feeling vocabulary is not very good. I went to schools for 21 years and I can't recall ever being asked how I felt, or what I needed, which is the next thing we're going to get to. No, I went to schools where the game was not at all concerned with what I was feeling and needing as a human being. The game was to get right answers. What you felt—people's feelings and needs—weren't part of the equation.

Part of the problem is the English language. Compared to other cultures in which I work, we have relatively few words for feelings.

Some other cultures I work in have a much richer vocabulary for feelings. I have a page of feeling words in English in my book, *Nonviolent Communication: A Language of Life*, to help people develop their feeling vocabulary. I've worked very hard to get this list together. And I was doing a workshop in a Spanish-speaking school and I noticed the teacher writing intensely on that page of feeling words. I went up during the break and looked at what she was writing and there, for every word in English, she was writing four or five Spanish variations.

Rollo May, the American psychologist, says that the mature human being has a feeling vocabulary, an ability to describe the life that's going on in them, that allows them to describe their life with all of the complexity of a symphony orchestra. And he said, sadly, that most of us walk around with a vocabulary in which we sound like a little tin whistle when it comes to talking about the life within us. So we haven't been taught to see the beauty in us. We've been taught to be good little boys, good little girls, good mothers, good fathers, good teachers, and that gets us disconnected from life. It gets us in our head. So the second step in Nonviolent Communication requires that we learn a vocabulary of feelings.

The next step involves being conscious of the cause of our feelings and to take responsibility for our feelings. The first two things I ask are "What did the other person do?" And then I say, "And how do you feel *when* they do this?" Notice I did not say, "How do you feel *because* they do it?" I'll now try to show you that the cause of our feelings is never what the other person does. What other people do is a stimulus for our feelings, but it can't cause our feelings. So what causes our feelings?

Incidentally, what I'm about to teach you, you already knew when you were six years old. You already knew that "sticks and stones can break my bones but..." What's the rest of it?

Let's say that I ask a child to do something, and the child says, "Leave me alone, stupid." Now, I know none of your students would ever speak to you that way, but some people tell me they actually have such people in their classroom. How do I feel about a student talking to me this way? Since other people can't make me feel anything, how I feel will depend on a choice that I make. What makes me feel as I do is my choice.

We knew when we were six that people couldn't make us feel

bad. It depended on how we took it. But then we were educated to believe that we can make other people feel as they do by guilt-inducing parents and teachers who said these things I've outlined before: "It makes me angry when you say that. That hurts me when you do that."

So if a child says to me, "Leave me alone, dummy," and I judge myself, I'll probably feel hurt. I'll take it as a criticism and I feel very bad. But I don't feel bad because they called me dummy. I feel bad because of how I took it.

Now, if instead I choose to judge the other, I feel mad, because now I'm telling myself this child is being disrespectful. That is no way for a child to talk to a teacher. But it's not the child calling me a name that makes me angry. I choose to look at it that way.

So some of us look inward and choose to take things personally. If we do, we'll spend a good deal of our life feeling guilty, shamed, and depressed. If we judge others we'll spend a good deal of our life being angry. And some of us are very talented. At one moment we can take in a statement like this and think, "Oh, I must be a bad teacher to have somebody talk to me that way," and we feel guilty or shamed, and then we flip around and get angry. We go through life vacillating between angry, guilty, shamed, depressed, angry, guilty, shamed, depressed.

Incidentally, those are very valuable feelings to a person using Nonviolent Communication: the feelings of anger, depression, guilt, and shame. Why are they valuable? All of those feelings tell us that we are dead. We're dead in this sense: We're cut off from where our attention really needs to be to see the beauty in ourselves and other people. And where do I suggest we place our attention? On the most important ingredient of Nonviolent Communication: needs.

On Needs

So another choice we can make is to see what need is at the base of our feelings. It's always a need. If we're really truthful, at the core it means a need of mine is not being met. So that's what we need to get good at, to connect our feelings to our needs, and to not express the feelings in a way that implies the other person has caused them. So whenever we say a feeling, "I feel frustrated, annoyed, angry, discouraged," the next two words are "because I."

We take responsibility for our feelings. "I feel because I . . ." "You feel because you . . ." If we mix those up in the language of the day, we blur boundaries, and start to play all kinds of *unfun* human games.

So what I'd like you to do now is develop your need vocabulary. I'd like you to say, "I feel as I do in this situation because I need . . ." So get connected to the need of yours that is not being met when the other person does what he or she does.

(Note: Again Marshall solicits ideas from the audience, which, along with his responses, have been included to help illustrate the concept of needs.)

What kind of needs did you get in touch with? (Taking responses from the audience) Need for acceptance, okay. A need for safety, yes. Other needs? Respect, yes. Approval? No. That's a dangerous one. You don't need approval. We want to keep needs separate from requests. We might request that somebody approve of what we do, but I'm going to suggest that we never mix up approval with gratitude. Are there more needs? Peace, yes. Safety, yes, those are all needs. A need for trust, a need to be able to depend on one another, yes. A need for love, yes. A giraffe uses the word love as a need. Jackals use the word love as a feeling.

For example, let me show you the difference between a jackal and a giraffe when it comes to love.

So since you used love as a need, we know you understand Nonviolent Communication. But if somebody says to you, "Do you love me," and you say, "Do you use the word love as a feeling?" Their response? "Well, yes, of course." Then you say, "Well, I just need to know that, I want to be honest. Because we don't use it as a feeling, we use it as a need. So now that I know you mean love is a feeling, ask it again."

"Do you love me?" And you say, "When?"

"When!?" "Well, yes, we want to be honest, and if you want to know my feelings, I can only answer at a given moment." "Well, what about right now?" "No. But try me again in a few moments, I might then."

Here's how a giraffe defines love. If you ask a giraffe, "So that's your need, love?" "Yes." And you ask a giraffe, "How can I meet that need?" And they'll say, "Speak giraffe."

What I'm sharing with you today is really what I've learned about love—how to live it. It's something you live, not something you feel. So I would say that we manifest love to the degree to which we openly reveal ourselves without criticizing others. And then the other half is how we respond to other peoples' messages to us. So I would say love is how we reveal ourselves, and how we receive other peoples' messages. That's the most powerful way I know of meeting needs for love.

So I have just taught you how to tell people "how you are" using Nonviolent Communication. This is a question that's asked all over the planet: "How are you?" Every culture that I work in, when people get together, they ask, "How are you?"

In a jackal culture it's asked, but people don't know how to answer, because they don't know a language of the heart. They don't know how to say how they feel, what they need. So the question becomes a ritual. But it's a very important question if we want to teach in a way that generates mutual respect. We need to evaluate from the heart, to really see how we are. And our training stresses to a large degree how both to express feelings and needs, and how to receive them.

On Requests vs. Demands

Now, after we have told people how we are, the next step requires expressing a clear request, and presenting a request as a request and not a demand. Demands are a losing game. The more important it is that somebody do something, the more important it is that they hear what you're asking as a request, not a demand. If people hear demands, it almost guarantees they will resist.

After you've spoken your feelings and needs, you would follow with a very clear request, what you want the other person to do. And your request needs to be stated in the positive, not the negative. That is, what you do want rather than what you don't want.

I was working with some teachers in Illinois. They were concerned at the number of broken windows in their school. And I said, "Okay, we got down to this point. Now, what do you want the students to do differently?" They said, "It's obvious. Quit breaking windows." I said, "You make my job as a consultant very easy when you tell me what you don't want." They said, "Really?

Well, what should we do?" "Kill them. Research demonstrates dead children break no windows." Now, don't go out and quote me as saying "kill children." I can see the headline: *Nonviolent Activist Suggests Killing Children Who Break Windows.*

What I was trying to show the teachers is that whenever we think of trying to get rid of a behavior, it makes violence look attractive. We need to get clear about the answers to those two questions I asked you earlier: What do you want, and more importantly, what do you want the person's reasons to be?

So we need to state our request in clear action language. Action language means we can't use vague words like "I want you to listen to me."

I had a husband and wife come to a workshop once. She said to him, "I want you to listen to me when I speak." He said, "I do." She said, "No you don't." He said, "Yes I do." They told me they'd had this same communication for 12 years. The problem was with the word "listen." It's too vague. So when we express our requests in Nonviolent Communication, they need to be very explicit.

And not only does it need to be explicit, but the other person needs to hear it as a request, not a demand. Now let me show you what happens if somebody hears a demand.

I was working in one school system on the east coast with a group of 40 students who were labeled socially and emotionally maladjusted. Now be honest with me. If you were in a class labeled socially and emotionally maladjusted, doesn't that give you permission to have fun in school? Labels lead to self-fulfilling prophecies. When we think students are slow learners, they will be. When we think people are socially and emotionally maladjusted, they will be.

So I knew already it was going to be a long day for me, just because of how these students were labeled. And it started as soon as I walked in the class. About half of the students were hanging out the window hollering obscenities at their friends in the courtyard down below. So I began by trying to make a clear request. I had to raise my voice to be heard. I said, "Would you all please come on over and sit down. I'd like to tell you who I am and what I'd like to do today." Half of them came over. I wasn't sure the other half heard me, so I repeated the request. Now everybody had come over except for two young men. I said to one of the young men, "Would you please tell me what you heard me say?" One of them said, "Yeah, you said we had to come over and sit down." See, that's the product of jackal schooling. He hears a demand already. Even though I make a request, he hears a demand.

So I said, "Sir," (I've learned always to use "sir" with people that have biceps like he had, especially with a tattoo on top of the bicep) "Sir, could you tell me how I could have let you know what I was wanting so it didn't sound like I was telling you what you had to do?" And he said, "Huh?" See, this is a major paradigm shift. It's harder for people to make the shift the longer they've been in jackal schools. So that's a big part of our training, to show teachers how to make our requests clear, so the person can trust it is a request and not a demand. Because once people hear demands, their options are submission or rebellion.

On Hearing Feelings and Needs—Empathic Connection

The other half of Nonviolent Communication, as I've already demonstrated by the story about my son, requires us to put on giraffe ears and learn how to hear any message that comes back at us as an expression of the other person's feelings and needs. Any message. So if the other person is silent, we don't hear the silence. With giraffe ears, we hear what this person might be feeling and needing behind the silence. If the other person says no, we don't hear it. We hear what the other person is feeling and needing. We have to guess. But we guess *human*. That's what Nonviolent Communication teaches us to do. No matter what message comes at us, we guess what this person might be feeling and needing.

For example, I was working with a group in a mosque in a refugee camp in Palestine. And when my translator said that I was an American, immediately a gentleman in the back jumped up and screamed at me at the top of his voice, "Murderer!" So what do I hear if someone calls me murderer? "See Me Beautiful." People need us to see the beauty in them the most when they're communicating in a way that makes it the hardest to see it in them. Like the student that says, "Leave me alone, dummy." Or like the student that isn't saying anything. That's when they need empathy the most. That's the accurate term for the receiving half of Nonviolent Communication. Empathic connection. For teaching purposes I use this little imagery, but it's a beautiful concept of empathy. Our training shows how to respond to any message with empathy.

So what did I hear when this person called me a murderer? I sensed what he was feeling. I sensed what he was needing. Even if you don't say anything, if your attention is there, immediately it transforms the dialogue. But in this case I checked it out. I wasn't sure I understood him. About an hour later he invited me to a Ramadan dinner at his house. And in that region we now have five giraffe schools in Israel, and four in Palestine.

But that came about when I heard him singing "See Me Beautiful" behind his message. So the other half of Nonviolent Communication is learning how to see whatever the other person is feeling and needing.

On Wonder and Green Jell-O

I would like to end today with a song made up of lines from young children that I work with. Very often in schools we teach the teachers how to teach Nonviolent Communication to the students. And one of the ways we do that is I go in and demonstrate it, and then I work with the teachers after school and show them how to teach it.

When I go in to teach Nonviolent Communication to students I like to start with this question: What do you wonder about? When I ask students that question during the day when I'm working with them, I'm bombarded with all kinds of things, and you'll hear their answers in this song. And after school I ask the teachers the same question. What do you wonder about? And you know the most typical response I get from teachers? Silence. And I say, "I wonder what happens to us between age six and now. You saw how the children responded. What happens to us?" And the teachers say, "Well, I was afraid that what I was wondering about would sound stupid." "I was afraid that what I was wondering about was abnormal." That's what happens to us. We lose our ability to wonder. We're educated in ways that make us worry about what we are, rather than what's alive in us.

So one day I asked a class of six year olds, and when the first boy responded, you could tell that this had been on his mind a long time. He said, "I wonder why my puppy won't eat green Jell-O with grapefruit in it." Most of the lines in this song came from the children.

Green Jell-O Song

I wonder why my dog won't eat green Jell-O
I like the wiggly way it melts inside
I wonder when a turtle pulls its head in
Is it so dark it's scared to be inside
I wonder if a rock likes being hard
I wonder if the sky likes being blue
I wonder if butterflies like butter
I wonder if you like being you

I wonder why I don't feel myself stretching
When people say I'm growing every day
I wonder why I always have to listen
To more words than I ever get to say
I wonder if the grass cries when it's cut
I wonder if the rain hurts when it falls
I wonder if the earth gets dizzy turning
I wonder if little worms feel small

I wonder why I see so many people
Do things that they don't really want to do
I wonder if the music goes away somewhere
After I sing my song to you
I wonder if it feels sad to be old
I wonder if the moon likes company
I wonder why it's fun to feel a little scared
I wonder if you wonder like me 2

Summary

Learning is too precious to be motivated by coercive tactics. NVC is interested in learning that's motivated by reverence for life, by a desire to learn skills, to better contribute to our own well-being and the well-being of others. The particular language that contributes to helping people learn by reverence for life is called, officially, Nonviolent Communication, but for teaching purposes it is sometimes called "Giraffe Language." Its opposite—"Jackal Language"—uses words such as "ought," "must," and "should." The basic vocabulary of Nonviolent Communication consists of feelings and needs.

It's important to develop a feeling and need vocabulary to assist in expressing oneself in NVC: "I feel (insert feeling) because I need (insert need)." Another basic concept in NVC is to distinguish between observation and evaluation. Observation is a clear and concise description of what is taking place. Any evaluation (judgment) of behavior is rendered in terms of feelings and needs, and by the principle of "power-*with*"—not "power-*over*"—people. Power-*over* leads to punishment and violence. Power-*with* leads to compassion and understanding, and to learning motivated by reverence for life rather than fear, guilt, shame, or anger. Power-*with* permits our needs to be heard as *requests* rather than demands. Demands result in defensiveness and refusal, while requests are more likely to be heard and accepted. After we've spoken our feelings and needs, we follow with a very clear request for what we want the other person to do. Requests are stated in the positive, in terms of what we do want rather than what we don't want.

In addition to expressing our needs and feelings, and expressing our needs as requests, Nonviolent Communication requires "empathic connection," to learn how to hear any message that comes back at us as an expression of the other person's feelings and needs. In short, Nonviolent Communication is a way of keeping our consciousness tuned in moment by moment to the beauty within others and ourselves.

---

1 "See Me Beautiful" by Kathy & Red Grammer © 1986, Smiling Atcha Music, Inc. Available from Red Note Records 800-824-2980

2 "Green Jell-O" by Ruth Bebermeyer

A Heart to Heart Talk

Introduction

In this excerpt from a workshop for Montessori educators given after the keynote presentation presented in the last section, Marshall enters into a role-playing exercise with a female teacher. He's asked her to bring to mind a person who's done something that doesn't make life wonderful for her. The purpose is to attempt to help participants learn and practice using Nonviolent Communication to express their feelings and needs, and to help them learn to connect empathically with the feelings and needs of others. Keep in mind the intention of Nonviolent Communication: to create the quality of connection that allows everyone's needs to be met and make life more wonderful for everyone. Marshall's words follow the letters MBR, while the female participant's words follow the letters FP.

•   •   •

MBR: Now, if you are to use Nonviolent Communication with this other person, you begin by saying to the person what the person has done that is not making life more wonderful for you. So, what did this person do that's not what you would like the person to do?

FP: My person is a three-year-old male, and he just grabbed a five-year-old by the throat and was choking him.

MBR: Wonderful. Now, what I haven't talked about previously is the use of force. When do you use force? I've said "no punishment," but I'm not suggesting that we at times do not use what we call "protective force." Nonviolent Communication requires being conscious of the difference between the *protective* use of force and the *punitive* use of force. There are times when we don't communicate, we act. This may be a case where I would act before I would

communicate. I would use force to stop it. I wouldn't hit—
that's the punitive use of force. But I might use force.
We're all in agreement so far: We act to stop behaviors that
are dangerous.

Conveying No Criticism

Now, what do we do with somebody who is behaving in a
way we don't like, if we would really like them to consider
another way of behaving? The first step I would recommend
is to sincerely communicate to this person that what they're
now doing is *the most wonderful thing in the world that
they could be doing.* So, if this person is beating on
somebody else and we would like to get this person to be
open to another way of meeting whatever needs are being
met, I'm suggesting the most powerful thing we can do to
begin our dialogue with this person is to communicate to
them in a way in which they feel absolutely no criticism for
what they're doing. Any criticism that this person hears
coming from our mouth would imply that what he is doing
is wrong, and will make it that much harder for him to
be open to learning a new possibility. So, how do we
communicate to this person that what they're now doing is
absolutely the most wonderful thing that they could be
doing? We listen using Nonviolent Communication to hear
what the person is feeling and needing. We tune in to what
message is being communicated through this person's
verbal and nonverbal communication. In this case the
communication is beating on somebody else. With
Nonviolent Communication we hear every message as an
expression of a feeling and a need. I've already mentioned
that if you want to get somebody to change their behavior
the first thing you need to do is communicate clearly and
sincerely that you understand why they're doing it in a way
that implies no criticism.

Here's a story that illustrates this point. Six months ago,
a woman in Switzerland came back to a workshop after
lunch and said, "Thank you, Marshall, for what you told me

this morning." She said, "I just tried it and really, I couldn't believe how profound the results were." I said, "You tried it?" and she said, "Yes, I called home during the lunch break. See, I've had a two-year struggle with my fifteen-year-old son. He's been smoking for two years. And for two years I have been trying to talk him out of smoking and the more I talked, the more he smoked, and I really understood what you meant by as long as you are trying to change somebody, if that's your objective, they'll resist it. So instead I called home and my thirteen-year-old answered the phone and I said, 'Where's your brother?' and he said, 'Out on the back porch.' Then I knew he was smoking, because at least we had agreed that if he was going to smoke he would not do it in the house. So, I said, 'Please get him for me.'" So, the son is on the phone and she says, "Your brother tells me you were out on the back porch smoking." "Yeah." "I learned something today in the workshop." "What's that?" "I learned that your smoking means that it's absolutely the most wonderful thing you could be doing." Well, that wasn't exactly how I had intended her to communicate. It's really through empathy that we demonstrate that, not by saying the words. But it worked for her, because he got it. I said, "What was his reaction?" She said, "It was profound given the way we've been arguing about this for two years. He hesitated for a long time when I said that and then he said, 'I'm not so sure about that.'" When people do not feel criticized, they don't have to put all of their energy into defense. They can start to look for some other option.

Our Objective—Empathic Connection to Help Meet Everyone's Needs

Now, there's a very important aspect of Nonviolent Communication I haven't mentioned. It's to ask: "What is our objective?" If our objective is to get what we want from the other person, that's not Nonviolent Communication. So, in this case it is not our objective to get this child to stop hitting other children. What is our objective? Our objective is to create the quality of connection that will allow everybody's needs to get met. For example, teachers will say, "How do I get a child to stop talking when I'm talking to the class?" I say, "As long as that's your objective the other person will probably not do it." As long as any human being of any age thinks you have single-mindedness of purpose, they'll probably resist. Or if they don't, and they do whatever you want, you'll probably pay for it. Many teachers or parents, when I say that their objective is never to get people to do what you want, assume that I'm talking about permissiveness, that you then just let the other person do whatever they want. Remember that I said that we need to create the quality of connection that will allow everybody's needs to get met. So, in this case—with this three-year-old—I'm suggesting that, in order to create the quality of connection that will allow everybody's needs to get met, I would start by empathically connecting with the feelings and needs being expressed in the child's actions. Can you do that now?

FP: This is why I got up here.

Hearing Feelings and Needs

MBR: When she is using Nonviolent Communication all she can hear is what this person is feeling and needing. Now that she's stopped the fight she's going to start the dialog—she's going to try to hear what the child is feeling and needing that's leading him to behave in such a way. She is not judging his behavior as right or wrong, good or bad. Her full attention is on "what is in this person's heart right now." Here's the words she's going to use: "Do you feel ____?" And she's going to guess what this person is feeling and she's going to add, "Because you need ____." She's going to hear the feelings and the needs being expressed through the message of beating on the other person. Let's start with that.

FP: Phillip, are you frustrated because you want the ball?

MBR: (Playing child's role.) "Yeah, he never gives it to me. He's always taking it from me. He never gives it to me."

FP: Now, I jump into my own style.

MBR: No, no, no. no.

FP: Is there another way?

MBR: It's much too early. We may have to go through four or five
or six more interchanges, because very often the first
message that we hear from another human being is but the
tip of the iceberg. And we never see the other messages
because we're too quick to jump in and become a "fix-it"
person. Let me show you what a fix-it person sounds like.
If they hear, "Nobody likes me," a fix-it person will respond
this way: "Well, I think it's because of the way you treat
others. Now if you treated others . . . " Right away they
want to jump in and educate.

    We're not ready yet to switch over. I ask many people
how many times when they have been in pain they recall
somebody being there to hear your feelings and needs.
And over half the people that I ask this question to can't
think of one time in their life. They can't recall one time
where they got what this student has already got: that
much empathy. And this is really my word for it.
Empathy: connecting with what a person is feeling and
needing. And when you do, the other person then has a
wonderful opportunity to explore it all.

    So, you've said, "Are you annoyed and wanting the
ball?" And he went deeper then that. He expressed more
then just this ball in this moment. He's saying that the other
boy never does anything, so this is a new message. This
also needs to be heard with empathy. So, what do you hear
now when he says, "You know, he never gives me the ball—
no one does. No one ever lets me play"?

FP: So, Phillip, are you feeling sad because you need to,
because you want to play with the other kids?

MBR: Yes.

FP: What else are you feeling, Phillip?

The Gift of Your Presence

MBR: Be careful of that kind of question. With that kind of question you're directing things. With empathy we don't direct, we follow. Don't *do* something, just be there. Your presence is the most precious gift you can give to another human being. Don't do something, just be there, just the way you were, just hearing feelings and needs. So just be there, just hear. He's really sad; he really has a need to be included that isn't being met. Now, if he doesn't seem to have anything further to say, maybe he can hear you. You can tell him how you feel now that you've heard him.

FP: Well, Phillip, I'm very concerned about the safety for the children on the playground.

MBR: Let me show you why that's not Nonviolent Communication. You expressed that you're in pain and you didn't end on a present request. Never express your pain to another human being without being explicit about exactly what response you want from them. If you just say what you did, the other person will think that you're trying to make them feel guilty because of how you feel. So, I like what you said so far, just don't stop. End on what you want from him at this moment.

Make Clear, Present Requests

Let me show you want happens when you express pain to another person, but you don't say what you want. I was on a train going to an airport, and as you get close to the airport, the train slows up; it goes very slow. This man was sitting across from me with his wife, and as soon as the train slows down he really gets in pain. And he says to his wife, "I have never seen a train go so slow in all of my life." Now, notice he's putting his pain out to another person, right? But he's not saying what he wants. It's a dangerous thing to do to just pour your pain out and not be clear what you want back. So, what does his wife do? She just sits there and looks tense. She wonders how to respond. And then she did what many of us do when we don't know, she just sat there, she didn't say anything. So, what does he do? Instead of being conscious that she's not responding because he didn't say what he wanted, he thinks that if he just repeats himself enough then he'll magically get his needs met. A second time he says to her, "I have never seen a train go so slow in all of my life." I loved her response, but I didn't think it was what he wanted. She said, "They're electronically timed." See, if we don't say clearly what we do need and what we do want back, we often get back a lot of crappy advice and information that we don't need or want. So, what does he do? You guessed it! A third time he says, "I have never seen a train go so slow in all of my life." Now she loses it. She says, "What do you want me to do? Get out and push?"

So, don't stop now, after you opened up your heart. You're concerned and you have a need for the safety of the playground. What is your clear, present request? What do you want back from him at this moment?

FP: Phillip, I'm concerned about the safety of the other children on the playground and I would like us to figure out a way together that you can play out here in the basketball court and other children will not be hurt.

MBR: Getting close, but notice the difference between "I'd like us to figure out" and "I'd like you to tell me."

FP: I'd like you to tell me what you need to be able to play out on this basketball court and be comfortable without other children getting hurt.

MBR: (Playing child's role.) "I don't know." But at least we're connecting. Maybe he doesn't know. But at least now we're ready to start looking for what might happen. Maybe you suggest something. What would you suggest?

FP: Phillip, I wonder if you can take another chance to think of any more ideas you have about what you could do besides touching somebody when you want the ball.

MBR: (Playing child's role.) "I don't know." You might suggest something to him, because while I think he's sincere, I don't think he really knows. He may only know violence and think of it as an option. I know many adults that don't know anything else to do except hit or they're just stumped what you do in a situation with conflict. You have to have a concrete suggestion.

FP: Well, Phillip, I know sometimes when I would like something I try to use my words. For example, I might say, "I notice that you have the yellow basketball and I was wondering if I could play with you?"

MBR: Now, the message you sent just now, was it received?

FP: No.

Checking to be Sure the Message is Received

MBR: It may or may not have been, you don't know. I would want to find out whether the message sent was message received, because I can tell you most adults would probably not hear that message for all kinds of reasons. So, I probably would've said, "I'd like you to tell me back what you heard me say so I can see if I made this possibility clear."

FP: So, Phillip, what do you think about that option of using your words?

MBR: (Playing child's role.) "I told him give me the ball, and he still wouldn't."

FP: I would go back to feelings. I would say, "I can see that you're still really frustrated that you wanted that ball."

MBR: "Yeah, and I did use words, but he didn't give me it."

FP: Well, Phillip, if you want to play on the basketball court, touching another child to get the ball is not an option.

MBR: But it is. He did it. He knows it's an option. Why would you lie to him?

FP: It's not an option that we have at this school.

MBR: But he knows he can do it. For example, I was working at a high school in the U.S., and one of the principals didn't like it when I said that human beings always have an option. They always have a choice. He said, "Then you obviously don't know the law in the state of Missouri. Children have to come to school until they are sixteen, there is no option." Now that was funny. And can you guess why it was funny? The board of education had hired me to work in this school because they had a thirty percent or greater unexplained absence rate each day. And here is the head of the school telling me that the students do not have an option about coming to school! Thirty percent knew they had an option.

Here is how you might say that message using Nonviolent Communication. Not that you don't have an option, but if you choose a given option, here's what I will do. Here we have to talk again about the protective use of force. I need to be clear that whatever I say is not intended to punish. That is not my intent—it's to protect. I have a need. I might say, "If I see you do this, here is what I will do." See, I'm not denying the other person has a choice. But, I'm letting them know the choice I will exercise.

FP: So, Phillip, I can see that you really want to play with the yellow basketball out on the basketball court and, for me, I don't feel comfortable having people use physical force to get the ball. If you choose that option then we will go inside and we can find something else to do.

MBR: Let me just check one other thing with this person. (Pretending to ask the child) "Could you tell me what the teacher was trying to tell you? How does the teacher feel about you hitting?" "She says I shouldn't do it." I didn't hear her say that. I heard her say that she is concerned because she had a need for the safety for other people, but it requires the other person use Nonviolent Communication to hear her feelings and needs. Just in the way he was listening to her, I wasn't still confident that he heard her feelings and needs. I think he felt understood by her, but I'm not confident that he heard her feelings and needs. That's why I asked him if he could tell me what the teacher's feelings and needs are. He hears he shouldn't have done it. As long as people hear that they shouldn't do something they will probably either continue doing it or stop doing it for a reason everybody will pay for later.

FP: So, can I ask you a question?

MBR: Yeah.

FP: This is not what happened with Phillip at all. Phillip grabbed another kid and I breathed ten times before I walked over. I said, "Phillip, can you tell me what just happened?" Phillip said, "I shouldn't squirt glue." And I said, "Well, I'm not concerned about glue right now, I'm concerned about people's safety." And he says, "I shouldn't run down the hallway." And he starts going through this . . .

MBR: Because he doesn't see the beauty in you. He's not seeing the beauty in you. He's seeing you as a "should-sayer." And as long as he sees you as a should-sayer, doing anything you want him to do is as enjoyable as a prolonged dental appointment. He's hearing you "should-ing" him. And as long as he hears you should-ing him he will resist what you want or do it with an energy that's not going to be good for anybody. Do you ever hear an adult say, "I shouldn't smoke, I should give up smoking, I should lose weight." What do they do? They resist it. We weren't born to be slaves. *Should* is slave language. Human beings resist shoulds. He's giving you a big message there when he says, "I shouldn't throw glue. I shouldn't hit the others." He didn't hear the beauty of what you said. He didn't hear your feelings and needs. So, you've got to make doubly sure he hears what you're saying rather then what he is used to hearing.

(Pretending to speak to the child) "So, Philip, I hear teacher being concerned because she has a need for everybody to be safe. Can you tell me what she said?" "I shouldn't hit kids." "Thank you for telling me that's what you heard. I heard her differently and to me it's really

important to hear her feelings." Until he sees her as a
human being it's no fun to do anything for her. "I heard her
say she's really scared and concerned. Could you say that?"
"Huh?" "I heard her say she's scared, concerned. Could you
say that back?" "She's scared and concerned." "I'd like you
to hear her needs. She has a need for everybody to be safe.
Could you tell me that back?" "She needs for everybody to
be safe." Now we've got a better connection. Now I think
it's going to be much easier to get the problem resolved.
You see, until that connection is there, until you've heard
this person's feelings and needs, until this person hears
your feelings and needs, if any demand gets in there, if any
criticism gets in there, it's going to be war and not a
resolution.

Now that he sees your need, I might say "So, is there a
way we can get your need to play with others and to get the
teacher's need for safety met?" "I don't know." "Well, I'd like
to go back over what the teacher said. How about asking the
students for the ball?" "I do. They don't give it to me." "I'd
like to hear how you ask." "I said, 'Give me the ball.'" "I'd like
you to look at another way of asking. Would you be willing
to look at another way of asking?" "They wouldn't give it to
me no matter how I asked for it." Again he is expressing a
message for which he needs understanding. "You feel pretty
discouraged about talking, so nothing is going to help." "No.
Nobody ever listens to me." "So, you feel kind of sad about
that. You'd really like people to listen to you, and you don't
know how to get them to." "No. My daddy doesn't listen to
me." "You feel real sad at home, too. You want people to
listen to you." "Yes." "I'm really glad you're sharing these
feelings with me. It helps me better understand that you feel
kind of hopeless about people ever just giving you
something because you want it." "Yeah." "Yeah, I'd like to at
least try what would happen if we ask for it differently.
Would you be willing to look at that with me?"

You notice I realized that I had to listen a lot more then
I did originally. There are a lot of feelings going on, a lot
of pain about not being listened to. And very often what I
predict you will find is that with just empathy, even if we

didn't solve it right now by finding another way, very often the hitting stops just with understanding of the pain behind the hitting. So, is there anything you want to say to Phillip while we're practicing?

FP: I would want to establish some kind of review or check in, or "let's try for another hour and then I'll come see how you're doing" or some kind of . . .

MBR: That check in might sound like, "Look, I'd like to suggest that you ask a little differently." How about just trying this: "Phillip, the next time you want something, instead of saying, 'Give me the ball,' how about, 'Would you be willing to give me the ball?' Would you just say that? Let's try that and then come back and tell me, and if that doesn't work and we'll try something else. Would you be willing to do that?" "Okay?" "Okay. And would you be willing to try that instead of hitting?" "Okay." You mean that kind of checking?

FP: Uh huh. And sometimes, I used to start out by saying, "Use your words, use your words," and then I realized that they didn't have any words to use. And I started telling them that when I'm in that situation I say this and then I have them practice on me and I found that really helped.

MBR: Of course. So, use your words, but some words make things worse. We have to say, "I would like to teach you how to speak in giraffe (use Nonviolent Communication) in those situations." And then we role-play, and we get them in these situations and show them how to express their feelings and needs; in fact we show them how to do the very thing that I was just showing you to do. We show them how to start by empathizing with why other people may not be giving them the ball. And then we show them how to express their pain in a way that is less likely to sound like a demand. So, anything else?

FP: So, Phillip, I really appreciate you standing here and taking the time and talking with me because I really want you to be able to have fun and for other people to be safe. So, thanks.

How Gratitude Can Feel Like a Judgment

MBR: Well, that's going to be hard for Phillip to take in because *one of the hardest messages for jackal-speaking people to hear is any expression of gratitude.* Especially when it's expressed in Nonviolent Communication, like the teacher did just now. I'd like to point out that she didn't jackal him and say, "You know, it's very good of you to do this." She didn't give him any compliment or praise. She spoke from the heart. She expressed her gratitude as her feelings and needs. Praise and compliments are very jackal, so if she had rewarded him with a positive judgment by saying, "You know, you're a very good student to talk about things like we did," that's just as violent language as to say "You're a bad student." But she didn't say that. She spoke from the heart. It's very hard for people who don't use NVC to hear gratitude expressed from the heart. Why? Because they've been living in a world that hears gratitude as a judgment. They wonder whether they deserved it or they wonder whether it's being used as a reward, because very often "thank you" is used as a reward, which is a sure way to spoil the beauty of gratitude.

So, he's afraid that this is just another manipulation. But the way she said it, it didn't sound like it. She was really coming from the heart, saying what she was feeling, that it met a need of hers to talk this way. So, that was pretty scary for him to take in. But I'm still glad the teacher said it, because even if it's hard for him to take in, he needs to hear it. I would even want to check it out to make sure. I might say, "Could you tell me what you heard me say just now about how I feel about our talk?" "That I should talk like this when there's a problem." "Well, thank you for telling me that's what you heard. I'd like you to hear me a little differently though. I'd like you to know how grateful I feel, because it meets a need of mine to be able to talk like this about things. Can you tell me that back?" "I don't know." "Well, it's important to me. Let me tell you again. Let me tell you the feelings. I really feel grateful. Could you say that back?" "You feel grateful." "Thank you. And it meets my need for connection with you so that we can connect. You know what I mean by connect?" "A little." "Well, I mean it meets my need to get along together. Could you tell me that back?" "Meets your need to get along." "Thank you for hearing that." See, it's just as important for me that people hear my appreciation as my messages of distress. I want to make sure they hear them both, and not hear my pain as a criticism and not hear my appreciation as a complement or as praise. Okay? Thanks for volunteering.

FP: Thank you.

Summary

The most powerful thing we can do to begin a dialog with a person with whom we have a conflict is to communicate with them in a way in which they feel absolutely no criticism for what they're doing. Our goal is to create a quality of connection (empathic connection) that allows everyone's needs to be met. We listen using Nonviolent Communication to hear what the person feels and needs. We tune in to the message being communicated through their verbal and nonverbal communication. With Nonviolent Communication we hear every message as an expression of a feeling and a need. Nonviolent Communication also requires being conscious of the difference between the *protective* use of force and the *punitive* use of force. We need to be clear that whatever we say is not intended to punish—that our intention is to protect. Instead of denying the other person's choice, we say what choice we will exercise. We express our needs in the form of clear, present requests. Praise, compliments, and expressions of gratitude are often heard as judgments. To create the quality of connection that is our goal it's just as important that people hear our appreciation as our messages of distress. It's often helpful to check with the other person to make sure the message given was the one received. And finally, even more than your words, your presence is the most precious gift you can give to another human being.

What's missing from this transcription is the experience of sharing time and space with Marshall Rosenberg or one of the Center for Nonviolent Communication certified trainers. The power, warmth, and poignancy of the NVC message are amplified by being at a training in person. The interplay with a live audience adds a dimension to the learning process that is hard to match on paper. If you'd like to see Marshall or another CNVC trainer in person, please visit www.CNVC.org for a schedule of NVC trainings and speaking engagements, and a listing of NVC trainers and supporters around the world.

LEARN MORE!
PuddleDancer Press

The premier publisher of Nonviolent Communication related works. Register for our quarterly e-newsletter, find media materials, and access hundreds of resources to learn and share NVC at: **www.NonviolentCommunication.org**

The Center for Nonviolent Communication

Find local, national and international training opportunities, trainer certification info, and a variety of other NVC educational materials at: **www.CNVC.org**

Bibliography

Craig, James and Marguerite. *Synergic Power.* Berkeley, CA: Proactive Press, 1974.

Holt, John. *How Children Fail.* New York: Pitman, 1964.

Katz, Michael. *Class, Bureaucracy and the Schools.* Preager Text Publishers, 2nd ed., 1975.

Katz, Michael. *School Reform: Past and Present.* Boston, Little, Brown & Co., 1971.

Mager, Robert. *Preparing Instructional Objectives.* Fearon Pub., 1962.

Milgram, Stanley. *Obedience to Authority.* New York: Harper and Row, 1974.

Postman, Neil and Weingartner, Charles. *Teaching as a Subversive Activity.* Delacorte, 1969.

Postman, Neil and Weingartner, Charles. *The Soft Revolution: A Student Handbook for Turning Schools Around.* New York: Delta, 1971.

Rogers, Carl. *Freedom to Learn.* Charles E. Merrill, 1969.

Rosenberg, Marshall. *Mutual Education: Toward Autonomy and Interdependence.* Seattle: Special Child Publications, 1972.

Some Basic Feelings We All Have

Feelings when needs "are" fulfilled

- Amazed
- Confident
- Energetic
- Glad
- Inspired

- Joyous
- Optimistic
- Relieved
- Surprised
- Touched

- Comfortable
- Eager
- Fulfilled
- Hopeful
- Intrigued

- Moved
- Proud
- Stimulated
- Thankful
- Trustful

Feelings when needs "are not" fulfilled

- Angry
- Confused
- Disappointed
- Distressed
- Frustrated

- Hopeless
- Irritated
- Nervous
- Puzzled
- Sad

- Annoyed
- Concerned
- Discouraged
- Embarrassed
- Helpless

- Impatient
- Lonely
- Overwhelmed
- Reluctant
- Uncomfortable

Some Basic Needs We All Have

Autonomy
- Choosing dreams/goals/values
- Choosing plans for fulfilling one's dreams, goals, values

Celebration
- Celebrate the creation of life and dreams fulfilled
- Celebrate losses: loved ones, dreams, etc. (mourning)

Integrity
- Authenticity • Creativity
- Meaning • Self-worth

Interdependence
- Acceptance • Appreciation
- Closeness • Community
- Consideration
- Contribute to the enrichment of life
- Emotional Safety • Empathy

Physical Nurturance
- Air • Food
- Movement, exercise
- Protection from life-threatening forms of life: viruses, bacteria, insects, predatory animals
- Rest • Sexual expression
- Shelter • Touch • Water

Play
- Fun • Laughter

Spiritual Communion
- Beauty • Harmony
- Inspiration • Order • Peace

- Honesty (the empowering honesty that enables us to learn from our limitations)
- Love • Reassurance
- Respect • Support
- Trust • Understanding

©CNVC. Please visit www.cnvc.org to learn more.

About CNVC

Founded in 1984 by Dr. Marshall B. Rosenberg, The Center for Nonviolent Communication (CNVC) is an international nonprofit peacemaking organization whose vision is a world where everyone's needs are met peacefully. CNVC is devoted to supporting the spread of Nonviolent Communication (NVC) around the world.

Around the globe, training in NVC is now being taught in communities, schools, prisons, mediation centers, churches, businesses, professional conferences and more. Dr. Rosenberg spends more than 250 days each year teaching NVC in some of the most impoverished, war-torn states of the world. More than 180 certified trainers and hundreds more teach NVC in 35 countries to approximately 250,000 people each year.

At CNVC we believe that NVC training is a crucial step to continue building a compassionate, peaceful society. Your tax-deductible donation will help CNVC continue to provide training in some of the most impoverished, violent corners of the world. It will also support the development and continuation of organized projects aimed at bringing NVC training to high-need geographic regions and populations.

CNVC provides many valuable resources to support the continued growth of NVC worldwide. To make a tax-deductible donation or to learn more about the resources available, visit their website at **www.CNVC.org**.

For more information, please contact CNVC at:

2428 Foothill Blvd., Suite E • La Crescenta, CA 91214
Phone: 818-957-9393 • Fax: 818-957-1424
Email: cnvc@cnvc.org • www.cnvc.org

About NVC

From the bedroom to the boardroom, from the classroom to the war zone, Nonviolent Communication (NVC) is changing lives every day. NVC provides an easy to grasp, effective method to get to the root of violence and pain peacefully. By examining the unmet needs behind what we do or say, NVC helps reduce hostility, heal pain, and strengthen professional and personal relationships.

NVC helps us reach beneath the surface and discover what is alive and vital within us, and how all of our actions are based on human needs that we are seeking to meet. We learn to develop a vocabulary of feelings and needs that helps us more clearly express what is going on in us at any given moment. When we understand and acknowledge our needs, we develop a shared foundation for much more satisfying relationships. Join the thousands of people worldwide who have improved their relationships and their lives with this simple yet revolutionary process.

About PuddleDancer Press

PuddleDancer Press (PDP) is the premier publisher of Nonviolent Communication™ related works. Its mission is to provide high quality materials that help people create a world in which all needs are met compassionately. PDP is the unofficial marketing arm of the international Center for Nonviolent Communication. Publishing revenues are used to develop and implement NVC promotion, educational materials and media campaigns. By working in partnership with CNVC, NVC trainers, teams and local supporters, PDP has created a comprehensive, cost-effective promotion effort that has helped bring NVC to thousands more people each year.

Since 2003, PDP has donated over 50,000 NVC books to organizations, decision-makers and individuals in need around the world. This program is supported in part by donations to CNVC, and by partnerships with like-minded organizations around the world. To ensure the continuation of this program, please make a tax-deductible donation to CNVC, earmarked to the Book Giveaway Campaign at www.CNVC.org/donation

Visit the PDP website at www.NonviolentCommunication.com to find the following resources:

- **Shop NVC** – Continue your learning—purchase our NVC titles online safely and conveniently. Find multiple-copy and package discounts, learn more about our authors and read dozens of book endorsements from renowned leaders, educators, relationship experts and more.

- **e-Newsletter** – To stay apprised of new titles and the impact NVC is having around the globe, visit our website and register for the quarterly NVC Quick Connect e-Newsletter. Archived newsletters are also available.

- **Help Share NVC** – Access hundreds of valuable tools, resources and adaptable documents to help you share NVC, form a local NVC community, coordinate NVC workshops and trainings, and promote the life-enriching benefits of NVC training to organizations and communities in your area. Sign up for our NVC Promotion e-Bulletin to get all the latest tips and tools.

- **For the Press** – Journalists and producers can access author bios and photos, recently published articles in the media, video clips and other valuable information.

- **NVC Community Forum** – Schedule for launch in 2005, the NVC Community Forum provides an online space to support the continued growth and spread of NVC worldwide. Join our forum today at www.ShareNVC.com

PuddleDancer PRESS

For more information, please contact PuddleDancer Press at:

P.O. Box 231129 • Encinitas CA 92024
Phone: 858-759-6963 • Fax: 858-759-6967
Email: email@puddledancer.com • www.NonviolentCommunication.com

Peaceful Living

Daily Meditations for Living with Love, Healing and Compassion

by Mary Mackenzie

$15.95 – Trade Paper 5x7.5, 390pp
ISBN: 1-892005-19-0

In this gathering of wisdom, Mary Mackenzie empowers you with an intimate life map that will literally change the course of your life for the better. Each of the 366 meditations includes an inspirational quote and concrete, practical tips for integrating the daily message into your life. The learned behaviors of cynicism, resentment, and getting even are replaced with the skills of Nonviolent Communication, including recognizing one's needs and values and making choices in alignment with them.

Peaceful Living goes beyond daily affirmations, providing the skills and consciousness you need to transform relationships, heal pain, and discover the life-enriching meaning behind even the most trying situations. Begin each day centered and connected to yourself and your values. Direct the course of your life toward your deepest hopes and needs. Ground yourself in the power of compassionate, conscious living.

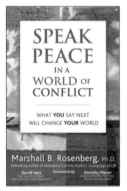

AVAILABLE FALL 2005
Speak Peace in a World of Conflict

What You Say Next Will Change the World

by Marshall B. Rosenberg, Ph.D.

$15.95 - Trade Paper 5-3/8x8-3/8, 240pp
ISBN: 1-892005-17-4

International peacemaker, mediator, and healer, Rosenberg shows you how the language you use is the key to enriching life. *Speak Peace* is filled with inspiring stories, lessons and ideas drawn from over 40 years of mediating conflicts and healing relationships in some of the most war torn, impoverished, and violent corners of the world. Find insight, practical skills and powerful tools that will profoundly change your relationships and the course of your life for the better.

Discover how you can create an internal consciousness of peace as the first step toward effective personal, professional, and social change. Find complete chapters on the mechanics of Speaking Peace, conflict resolution, transforming business culture, transforming enemy images, addressing terrorism, transforming authoritarian structures, expressing and receiving gratitude, and social change.

Bestselling author of the internationally acclaimed,
Nonviolent Communication: A Language of Life

Available from PDP, CNVC, all major bookstores, and Amazon.com
Distributed by IPG: 800-888-4741

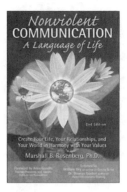

Nonviolent Communication:
A Language of Life, Second Edition

Create Your Life, Your Relationships and Your World in Harmony with Your Values

Marshall B. Rosenberg, Ph.D.

$17.95 – Trade Paper 6x9 • 240pp
ISBN: 1-892005-03-4

In this internationally acclaimed text, Marshall Rosenberg offers insightful stories, anecdotes, practical exercises and role-plays that will literally change your approach to communication for the better. Nonviolent Communication partners practical skills with a powerful consciousness to help us get what we want peacefully.

Discover how the language you use can strengthen your relationships, build trust, prevent or resolve conflicts peacefully, and heal pain. Over 100,000 copies of this landmark text have been sold in 20 languages around the globe.

"Nonviolent communication is a simple yet powerful methodology for communicating in a way that meets both parties' needs. This is one of the most useful books you will ever read."
— **William Ury**, co-author of *Getting to Yes* and author of *The Third Side*

"I believe the principles and techniques in this book can literally change the world, but more importantly, they can change the quality of your life with your spouse, your children, your neighbors, your coworkers and everyone else you interact with."
— **Jack Canfield**, author, *Chicken Soup for the Soul*

Nonviolent Communication
Companion Workbook

A Practical Guide for Individual, Group or Classroom Study

by Lucy Leu

$19.95 – Trade Paper 7x10 • 224pp
ISBN: 1-892005-04-2

Learning Nonviolent Communication has often been equated with learning a whole new language. The *NVC Companion Workbook* helps you put these powerful, effective skills into practice with chapter-by-chapter study of Rosenberg's cornerstone text, *NVC: A Language of Life*. Create a safe, supportive group learning or practice environment that nurtures the needs of each participant. Find a wealth of activities, exercises and facilitator suggestions to refine and practice this powerful communication process.

Available from PDP, CNVC, all major bookstores, and Amazon.com
Distributed by IPG: 800-888-4741

Additional NVC Books from PuddleDancer Press

 NEW! Being Me, Loving You • *A Practical Guide to Extraordinary Relationships* by **Marshall B. Rosenberg, Ph.D.** • Discover the "how-to" of heart to heart connections strengthened by joyfully giving and receiving. 80pp, ISBN: 1-892005-16-6 • **$6.95**

AVAILABLE FALL 2005! Eat by Choice, Not by Habit • *Practical Skills for Creating a Healthy Relationship with Your Body and Food* by **Sylvia Haskvitz** • Let NVC help you uncover the missing link in your relationship with your body and food. 128pp, ISBN: 1-892005-20-4 • **$8.95**

Getting Past the Pain Between Us • *Healing and Reconciliation Without Compromise* by **Marshall B. Rosenberg, Ph.D.** • Learn the healing power of listening and speaking from the heart. Skills for resolving conflicts, healing old hurts, and reconciling strained relationships. 48pp, ISBN: 1-892005-07-7 • **$6.95**

The Heart of Social Change • *How to Make a Difference in Your World* by **Marshall B. Rosenberg, Ph.D.** • Learn how creating an internal consciousness of compassion can impact your social change efforts. 48pp, ISBN: 1-892005-10-7 • **$6.95**

Parenting From Your Heart • *Sharing the Gifts of Compassion, Connection, and Choice* by **Inbal Kashtan** • Addresses the challenges of parenting with real-world solutions for creating family relationships that meet everyone's needs. 48pp, ISBN: 1-892005-08-5 • **$6.95**

NEW! Practical Spirituality • *Reflections on the Spiritual Basis of Nonviolent Communication* by **Marshall B. Rosenberg, Ph.D.** • Marshall's views on the spiritual origins and underpinnings of NVC, and how practicing the process helps him connect to the Divine. 48pp, ISBN: 1-892005-14-X • **$6.95**

Raising Children Compassionately • *Parenting the Nonviolent Communication Way* by **Marshall B. Rosenberg, Ph.D.** • Filled with insight and stories, this booklet will prove invaluable to parents, teachers, and others who want to nurture children and themselves. 32pp, ISBN: 1-892005-09-3 • **$5.95**

NEW! The Surprising Purpose of Anger • *Beyond Anger Management: Finding the Gift* by **Marshall B. Rosenberg, Ph.D.** • Learn the key truths about what anger is really telling us. Use it to uncover your needs and get them met in constructive ways. 48pp, ISBN: 1-892005-15-8 • **$6.95**

Teaching Children Compassionately • *How Students and Teachers Can Succeed with Mutual Understanding* by **Marshall B. Rosenberg, Ph.D.** • Skills for creating a successful classroom—from a keynote address and workshop given to a national conference of Montessori educators. 48pp, ISBN: 1-892005-11-5 • **$6.95**

We Can Work It Out • *Resolving Conflicts Peacefully and Powerfully* by **Marshall B. Rosenberg, Ph.D.** • Practical suggestions for fostering empathic connection, genuine cooperation, and satisfying resolutions in even the most difficult situations. 32pp, ISBN: 1-892005-12-3 • **$5.95**

What's Making You Angry? • *10 Steps to Transforming Anger So Everyone Wins* by **Shari Klein and Neill Gibson** • A step-by-step guide to re-focus your attention when you're angry, and create outcomes that are satisfying for everyone. 32pp, ISBN: 1-892005-13-1 • **$5.95**

Available from PDP, CNVC, all major bookstores and Amazon.com. Distributed by IPG: 800-888-4741. For more information about these booklets or to order online visit www.NonviolentCommunication.com